Crochet

25 Easy Patterns for Beginners

A Step-By-Step Guide to Mastering the Basics While Having Fun

Lindsay Moore

Introduction

I want to thank you and congratulate you for buying the book, *"Crochet – 25 Easy Patterns for Beginners"*.

In today's society it is increasingly hard to come across activities that do not include technology and our hobbies are no exception. For the most part our hobbies have lost their traditional purpose of relaxing, connecting with others and expressing ourselves in ways that reflect our interests, creative or otherwise. Nowadays, people's 'hobbies' tend to focus on engaging in activities such as social media, online gaming, watching Netflix or other distractions that do not require much mental dexterity or promote a sense of community.

You might think that hobbies such as crocheting are outdated, but they are quite beneficial! Not only are these creative hobbies fun but they help in stimulating your mind and can be a great way to manage stress and promote happiness.

In this book, you will learn the basics of the art of crochet, including an outline of the tools you will need, an overview of the types of stitches to use and basic instructions for 25 easy patterns that any beginner can start doing.

Finally, we will address common mistakes that beginners make and provide you with practical tips to get started right away.

Thanks again for buying this book. I hope you enjoy it!

© Copyright 2019 by Lindsay Moore - All rights reserved.

This document is geared towards providing exact and reliable information in regard to the topic and issue covered. The publication is sold with the idea that the publisher is not required to render accounting, officially permitted, or otherwise, qualified services. If advice is necessary, legal or professional, a practiced individual in the profession should be ordered.

- From a Declaration of Principles which was accepted and approved equally by a Committee of the American Bar Association and a Committee of Publishers and Associations.

In no way is it legal to reproduce, duplicate, or transmit any part of this document in either electronic means or in printed format. Recording of this publication is strictly prohibited and any storage of this document is not allowed unless with written permission from the publisher. All rights reserved.

The information provided herein is stated to be truthful and consistent, in that any liability, in terms of inattention or otherwise, by any usage or abuse of any policies, processes, or directions contained within is the solitary and utter responsibility of the recipient reader. Under no circumstances will any legal responsibility or blame be held against the publisher for any reparation, damages, or monetary loss due to the information herein, either directly or indirectly.

Respective authors own all copyrights not held by the publisher.

The information herein is offered for informational purposes solely, and is universal as so. The presentation of the information is without contract or any type of guarantee assurance.

The trademarks that are used are without any consent, and the publication of the trademark is without permission or backing by the trademark owner. All trademarks and brands within this book are for clarifying purposes only and are the owned by the owners themselves, not affiliated with this document.

Table of Contents

Understanding Crochet 1
    The Origin and History of Crochet 1
    Crochet Projects 2
Why Crochet As A Hobby 3
Materials Needed For Crochet 6
    Yarn 6
    Hooks 9
Crochet Terms and Abbreviations 16
Basic Crochet Stitches 20
    Slip Stitch (sl st) 20
    Chain Stitch 22
    Single Crochet 24
    Half Double Crochet 26
    Double Crochet 27
    Treble Crochet Stitch 30
Easy Crochet Patterns for Beginners 33
Common Mistakes in Crochet and How to Avoid Them 88
Crochet Tips for Beginners 92
Conclusion 94

Understanding Crochet

Crocheting is simply the process of creating fabric by intertwining loops of thread, yarn wire, twine or strands of other types of innovative material using a crochet hook. The name 'crochet' is derived from a French word 'croche', which literally translates to hook. In French, crochet means small hook. The hooks used in crocheting are usually made of materials such as plastic, wood or metal.

The Origin and History of Crochet

The reality of the history of crochet is that no one can pinpoint the exact time when it was invented or by whom. However, there is a lot of information of its discovery, and its spread to various parts of the world.

Knitted textiles can be traced from the early ages (as early as 1500-1800 BC) but the first substantial evidence of the existence of crocheted fabric relates to its appearance during the 19th century in Europe where it was known as 'shepherds knitting'. The word crochet first appeared in 1823 in the Dutch magazine *Penélopé*. It contained the first known published instructions for crochet, which explicitly used that term in designating the craft in its present sense. The earliest dated English mention of garments made of cloth that was produced by looping yarn using a hook is The Memoirs of a Highland Lady written by Elizabeth Grant.

Notwithstanding a pure British origin, solid evidence was uncovered of a connection between crochet and French tambour embroidery. In 1763, crochet was illustrated in detail in Diderot's Encyclopedia. The use of steel needles, wooden hooks, bone and ivory has been frequently mentioned in several other books.

Crochet Projects

Popular projects include tote bags, purses, shawls, granny squares, hats, scarves, baby booties, baby blankets, Afghans and many others. You can also crochet a variety of other different things such as curtains, socks and jewellery.

It's also possible to crochet various components to use in making other items. For example, crochet edgings and trimmings, which can be used on knitted items, crocheted items and even sewn items (including finished store-bought items). For instance, you could purchase pillowcases, towels and/socks then add a crocheted edging to each

Why Crochet As A Hobby

Among all the hobbies there are, why bother with crocheting? Well, let us find out:

Crocheting can Reduces Stress and Anxiety

When you crochet, you need to be in the moment and concentrate on your work or you will end up messing everything, which can be a lot of work trying to undo. This ability to be in the moment working on something enables you not to have too many thoughts racing through your mind. Your mind is able to free itself from anxious ideas or thoughts and be more relaxed when you focus on counting rows, and the repetitive motions of individual stitches.

Helps Relieve or Ease Depression

Whenever we do something that we like or enjoy, our brain releases a chemical known as dopamine, which affects emotions like a natural anti-depressant. According to scientists, crafts such as crocheting may help in stimulating the release of dopamine thereby allowing you to feel happier. Furthermore, you derive great satisfaction when you see the progress in your work and when you finally finish a project, which makes you feel great about yourself.

Helps with Insomnia

When you focus your mind on something that is easy, soothing and repetitive such as crochet, it helps in calming your mind and body enough to allow you to fall asleep. Therefore, the next time you are having a hard time getting some sleep, don't get frustrated, just pick up your tools and crochet and before long, you will feel sleepy.

Builds your Self-Esteem

We all want to feel useful and productive and by working on a crochet project to sell at a craft fair or give as a gift, we can just do that. This does not necessarily mean that we crochet to fish for compliments, however, a little external validation by your gift recipient wearing the scarf or mittens you made through winter or someone buying your finished item can give you the boost of self-esteem that you need.

Crocheting Reduces the Risk of Alzheimer's by 30-50%

By stimulating your mind and engaging in cognitive exercises, you can slow down or prevent memory loss. Whether you are challenging your memory by simply reading, trying out a pattern or learning a new technique or stitch, getting a little crafty helps you to preserve your memory.

Crocheting Puts You in Control

Whether you are feeling helpless watching someone struggle or you are the one struggling with your own problems or illness, crocheting is a great way to put back the control into your hands - literally. When you chose to create, you are in full control of everything, from the project type, the type of crochet hooks and even the type and color of yarn you will be using. This makes all the difference in the world, as it makes you feel like you finally have a say.

Crocheting Acts as a Form of Group Therapy

Working on a project in a group helps those in the group to have an immediate way of relating to the other group members and can work as an ice breaker for more serious discussions or conversations. Even if you are not seeking therapy actively, you can enjoy the sense of community brought about by crocheting.

Materials Needed For Crochet

Basics: You only need yarn/thread, crochet hooks and scissors to start crocheting.

Yarn

You can use a variety of yarns to crochet but the type of yarn you chose depends on the type of project. You can crochet with any kind of yarn, even non-fiber yarn-like materials. While you can use any type of yarn, as a beginner, you will find it best to use the yarn options we will outline below since they are easier to work with than others are.

Choosing the Best Yarn for Crochet

Fiber type

This is the first decision you have to make as you embark on your crochet journey. There are quite a number of options to choose from for both plant and animal fibres. However, we will focus on the three most common and basic ones: acrylic, cotton and wool.

You might be wondering how to know which type of fiber you are working with but it's really quite simple – the type of fiber is usually listed on the yarn label. Although as you familiarize yourself with crocheting, you will find yourself being able to identify the fiber type by just handling or even looking at the yarn.

Acrylic yarn: Acrylic is generally a popular yarn among crochet enthusiasts. It is usually among the affordable choices for yarn, comes in a variety of colors and is widely available. It is a more-than-acceptable choice for you as a beginner. However, you should be aware that some of the cheapest acrylics split apart thereby making it quite challenging to work with. This case is not usually common but it does happen. Therefore, if you are having a hard time working with acrylic, try switching to a different brand or you can just use wool or cotton instead.

Cotton yarn: It's an inelastic fiber thereby making it a bit more challenging to work with than wool. However, where you want the item to hold its shape, this quality makes cotton a great choice for specific projects. Although some may find it a bit more challenging than wool, it is not that different at all and it is something you can certainly try as a beginner. If you are crocheting during summer where working with wool is unpleasant due to the heat, cotton is a great choice since its lighter than wool.

Wool Yarn: Wool is the perfect choice for you to practice your stitches. It is forgiving of mistakes and is a resilient fiber. If you happen to make a mistake while crocheting, most wool yarns, are easy to unravel and even re-use (in crochet, it's called frogging). Wool yarn is not suitable for those with wool allergies but for most, it is a good crocheting choice.

Additional Yarn Tips and Considerations

Yarn weight: Yarns come in different thicknesses as well. This thickness is what we refer to as weight. The weight of the yarn is usually found on the label where it's numbered 1-7 (from the thinnest to the thickest). It is easiest to work with a worsted weight yarn as a beginner, which is #4 on the yarn label.

Note: it is advisable that you use the correct crochet hook size for the yarn weight you will be using.

Yarn color: Choose lighter yarn colors rather than dark ones, as it can get challenging to see your stitches if using yarns with dark colors.

Yarn texture: Choose smooth yarn and not the textured ones. As you begin crocheting, avoid eyelash yarns and any other textured novelty yarns, which can get quite frustrating to work with.

Yarn yardage: Each ball of yarn has different yardage amounts, which relates to the price. You can find 2 balls of yarn with the same price; just check the yardage to ensure the amount of yarn in each ball is approximately the same.

Yarn price: The price of yarn varies significantly from brand to brand and fiber to fiber. It is better to work on the affordable ones so that you get the hang of it before investing a lot of money in very expensive yarns. This is why acrylic, wool and cotton are the top fiber choices, as they tend to be the most affordable.

Yarn color dye lot: If you want to crochet a large project that will need more than 1 ball of yarn, then you want to ensure that all the colors match (assuming that you are using the same color-way or color for the entire project). You do this by checking the "dye lot on the yarn label to ensure that the balls are from the same dye lot number so that they don't have noticeable differences between them.

Washing details: Different fiber types have different washing instructions, which will be really important if you are crocheting something to wear. For instance, you can use superwash wool that is safe to put in the washer and dryer or you can go so for some type of wool that must be hand washed and dried flat because it will shrink in the dryer. The yarn label contains this information to aid in your selections.

Hooks

The average crochet hook works for anyone and it definitely favours beginners like you. You will find crochet hooks sold at yarn stores or any major craft retailer. You can also get them online. Below are a few things you need to know about crochet hooks:

Material: A basic crochet hook can be made of several common materials such as bamboo, plastic and aluminum. Most people usually choose aluminum crochet hooks for their first project. There are also fancier crochet hooks made of wood, glass, and clay.

Size: Crochet hooks differ in size; there are many different sizes which are measured in numbers, letters or millimetres. For instance, a basic crochet hook set may range from E – J. A general-sized crochet hook is normally H-8 5mm. Size E is smaller than size H, size J is larger. As mentioned earlier, you should match the size of your crochet hook with the weight of your yarn, which is usually on the label of the yarn. For most beginners, it is usually advisable to work with a size G or H crochet hook and worsted weight yarn.

Hook throat: A crochet hook has either an inline or tapered "throat", resulting in less or more flatness to the head of the hook. Since neither is better than the other is, if you find it hard to work with one, just try the other.

Types of Crochet Hooks

Let us now look at the various types of crochet hooks at your disposal as you get started:

Thread Crochet Hooks

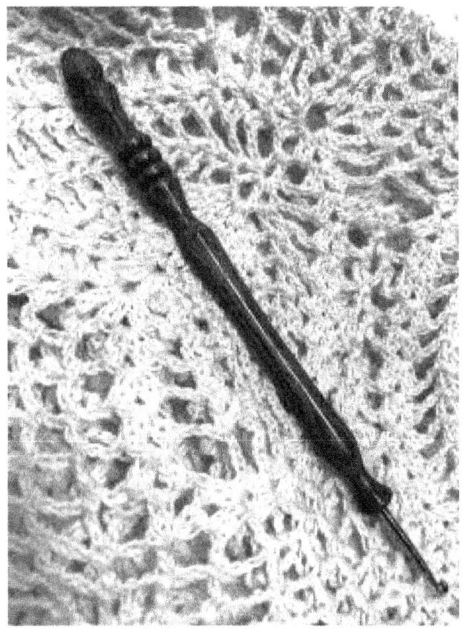

When you are using thread to crochet instead of yarn, the crochet hook you use is similar but it is quite smaller than a yarn hook. The hooks are also usually made of steel in order to prevent bending while you crochet, a problem that is less popular among larger hook sizes.

Light-up crochet hooks

If you suffer from insomnia or if you simply want to crochet in the middle of the night without being a bother to anyone, then light-up crochet hooks are what you need.

They light up at the tip so that it is easier to see where you are going to insert the hook to crochet. They are typically regular crochet hooks that light up.

Ergonomic crochet hooks

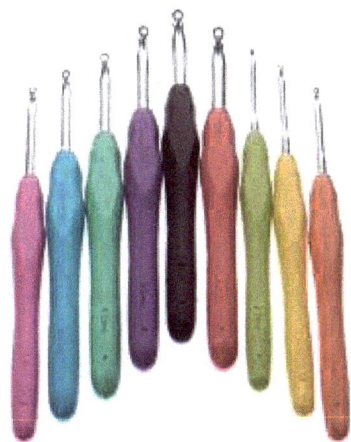

Sometimes it can become quite uncomfortable to crochet with regular hooks for a long time especially if you suffer from hand conditions such as arthritis or carpal tunnel. Fortunately, there are ergonomic crochet hooks, which have larger handles that are shaped to create a grip that makes it easier to crochet for long.

Tunisian crochet hooks

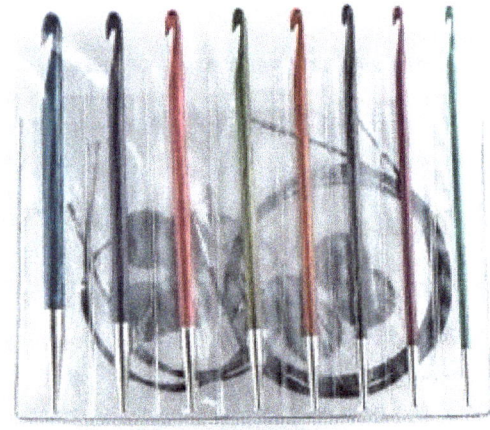

Tunisian crochet is a niche of crocheting that uses a completely different set of stitches from regular crocheting. Tunisian crochet hooks are also known as Afghan crochet hooks and are longer than the regular crochet hooks. These hooks can have a cable to connect a one-headed hook to another one-headed hook or they can have a head on either side of the hook.

Knook

A knook looks like a regular crochet hook but it has a small hole drilled into one end where you insert the thread for holding your stitches.

Crochet Terms and Abbreviations

Alt = alternate

Beg = means beginning, like the beginning of the row

Bp = means "back post" like rather that working through the loops, you are working the stitch around the post. You typically pair it with the abbreviation of the stitch you are using. For example, bpdc stands for back post double crochet whereas bpsc stands for back post single crochet

BL = refers to "back loop" crochet. It might also be seen as BLO "back loop only". Occasionally BL can also be used to refer to bobbles or blocks, specific to the pattern using it. For this information, check the stitch list of the pattern that is usually found at the beginning of the pattern.

BO = Bobble

cl = cluster. Your pattern should specify the type of cluster being used, as there are many different types of clusters. For instance, 3 tr cluster refers to a cluster of 3 treble crochet stitches

ch(s) = chain(s). This is one of the most common abbreviations you will see since almost all crochet patterns start with chains. Most patterns also include chains throughout the design.

dtr = double treble crochet

dec = decrease. It's a technique used for shaping in crochet

dc = double crochet. It's one among the most common basic crocheting stitches

incl = inclusive / including / include

inc = increase. It's another technique used in shaping, like dec (decreasing) is used

hdc or half dc = half double crochet. Its a basic crochet stitch in between double crochet and single crochet in height

FP = front post as compared to "back post" explained above

FL = front loop. It is also abbreviated as FLO (front loop only) in contrast to BL/BLO as earlier mentioned

PM = place marker

Pc = popcorn. A textured crochet stitch that is similar to bobbles and clusters. Patterns that use these types of stitches normally explain how the designer wants to make the stitch at the beginning of the pattern where the crochet abbreviation preferred by the designer will also be seen

Rem = remaining

Dc = Double crochet

Dtr = Double treble crochet

oz = ounce(s). It's likely to be seen in the portion of the patterns of crocheting explaining how much yarn is required or on yarn labels. It may also be measured in other ways such as yards (yd), meters (m) or grams (g)

RS = right side. When worked in rows, crochet has both right side and wrong side

rnd(s) = round(s). They are used for counting when working in the round or otherwise working in circles (in contrast to working in rows)

rev = reverse. It is typically used together with other abbreviations such as rev sc, which means reverse single crochet stitch

rep = repeat. It is frequently placed together with symbols that show the portion of the patter that is going to be repeated. Examples:

- [] = the pattern specifies the times to repeat a series of instructions given inside the brackets
- () = the pattern specifies the times to repeat a series of instructions given inside the parentheses
- * = the pattern specifies the times to repeat a series of instructions given between asterisks or following an asterisk

st(s) = stitch(es)

sp(s) = space (s)

sl st = slip stitch. It's the method used in joining rounds when crocheting as well as a stitch that is used on its own

sk = skip. For instance, you can skip the next chain and work into the one following which will be indicated by the term sk ch (skip chain)

sc = single crochet. It is one of the most basic and frequently used crochet stitches

tr = triple crochet/ treble crochet. Its another basic crochet stitch

tr tr = triple treble crochet. Another tall crochet stitch is even taller than the dtr described earlier

tog = together. It is sometimes used to replace dec(rease) where it can be written as "sc2tog" to mean a decrease in single crochet stitch

WS = wrong side. It's the opposite of right side (rs) as earlier described

WIP = work in progress.

Yoh = yarn over hook

YO = yarn over. A step is used in making most crochet stitches. It's typically not seen in crochet patterns but is often seen in crochet stitch tutorials

Basic Crochet Stitches

This chapter will focus on some of the basic crochet stitches that you are likely to come across:

Slip Stitch (sl st)

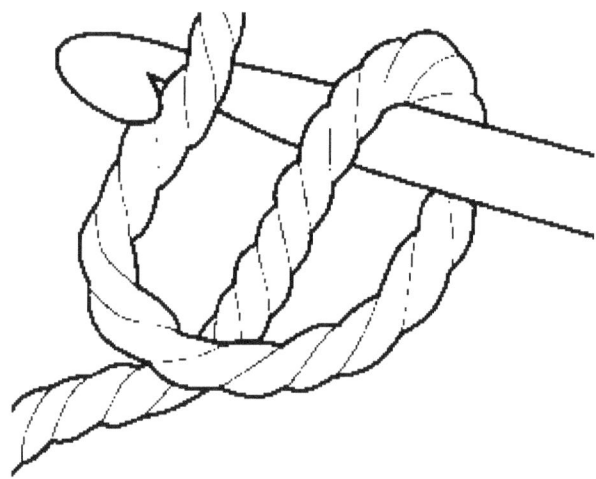

1. Using your yarn, make a loop and insert the hook into the loop.
2. Hook another loop through the first one.
3. Tighten the slip knot and slip it up your hook and you have a slip knot or slip stitch.

Chain Stitch

1. YO, draw the yarn through the slip knot to form a chain stitch.

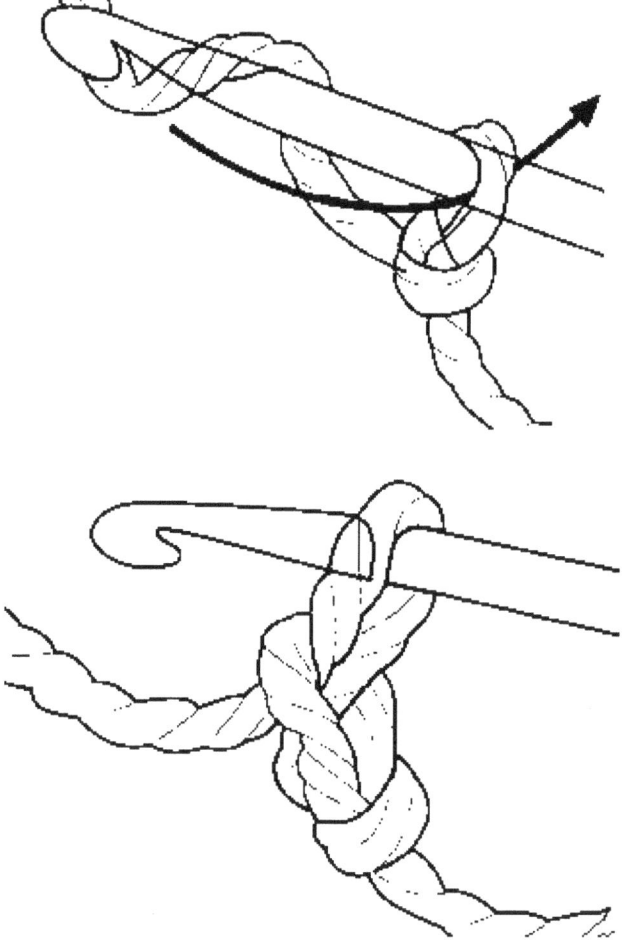

2. Repeat and have as many chain stitches as you want.

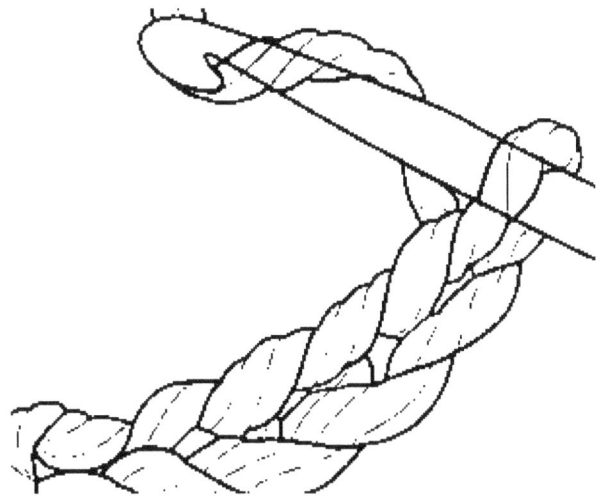

Note: Do not count the slip stitch or slip knot as a chain stitch.

Single Crochet

1. Insert your hook into the 2nd chain from the beginning chain.

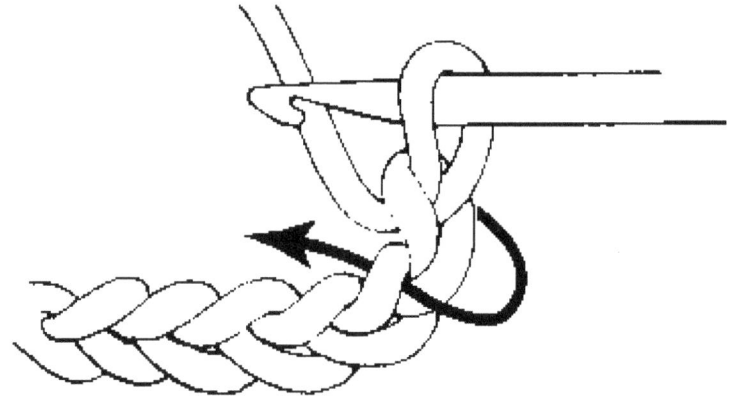

2. YO and draw it through the chain stitch and there will be two loops.

3. Yarn over and into the two loops and you have a single crochet.

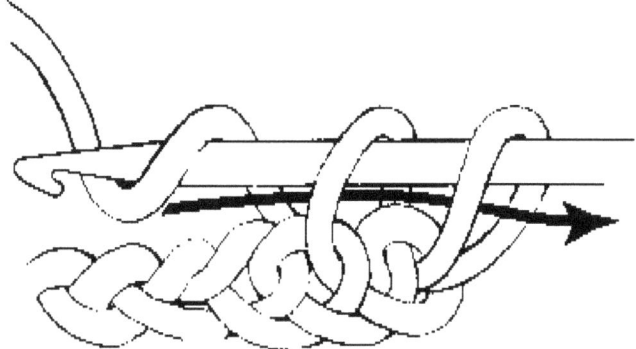

4. Insert your hook into the following stitch and repeat the steps above for the number of single crochet stitches you want.

Half Double Crochet

1. YO your hook and into the third chain from the hook.

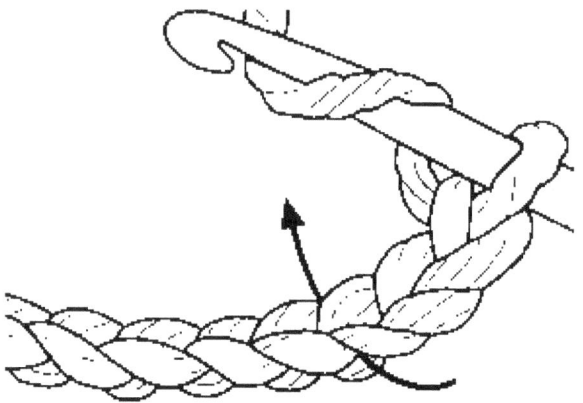

2. Yarn over and into the third chain and you will have three loops.

3. YO and into the three loops; that is a half double crochet stitch.

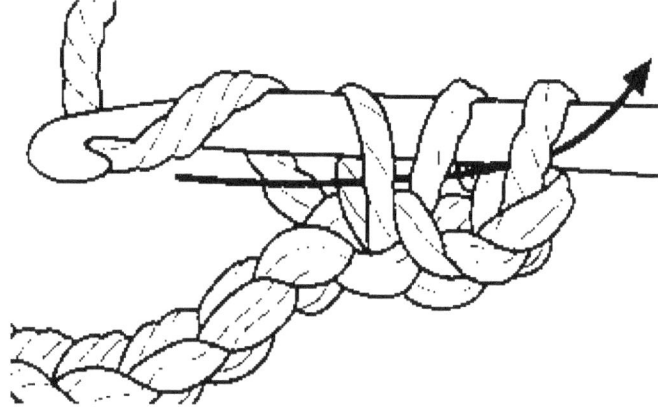

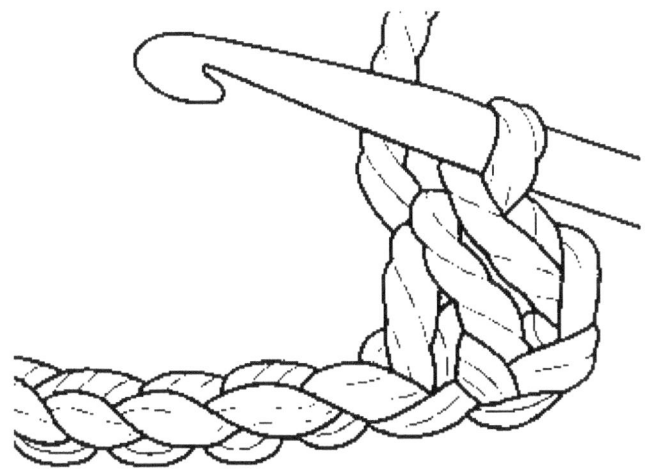

4. YO, insert your hook into the following chain and repeat from step 2.

Double Crochet

1. YO and insert it into the 4th chain from the beginning chain. YO and draw it through the chain; you will now have three loops.

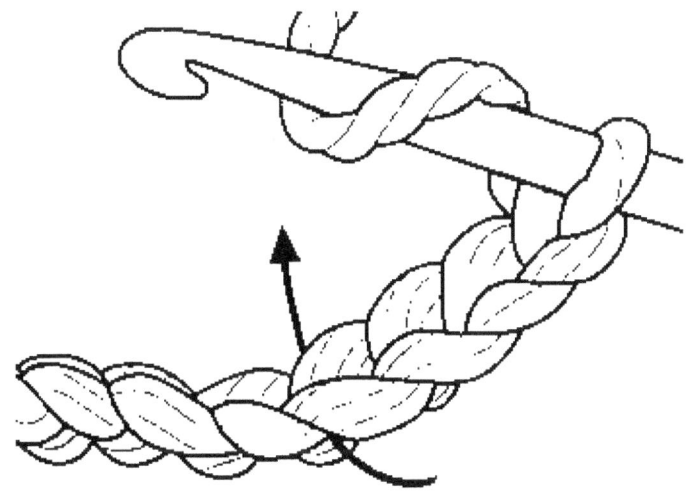

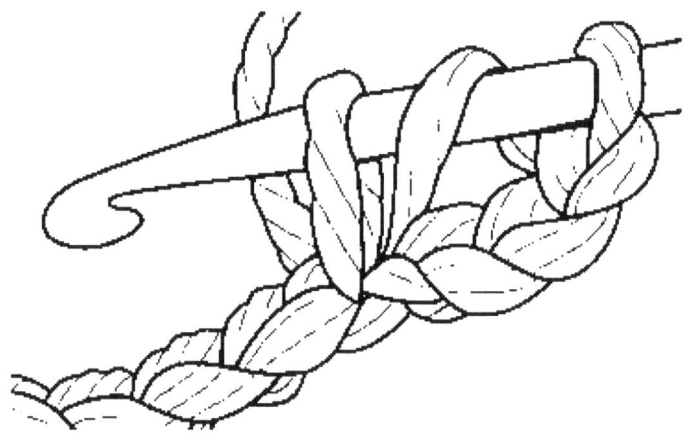

2. YO and draw through the first two loops only; you will now have two loops.

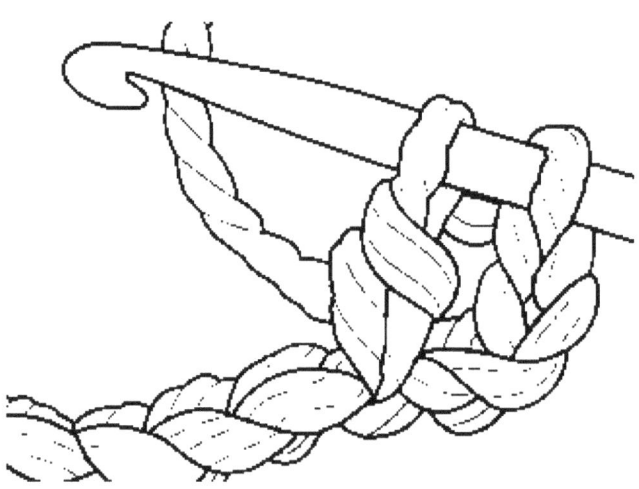

3. YO and into the last two loops; this is one double crochet.

4. YO and insert into the following stitch; repeat the steps above.

Treble Crochet Stitch

1. YO twice and insert the hook into the fifth stitch.

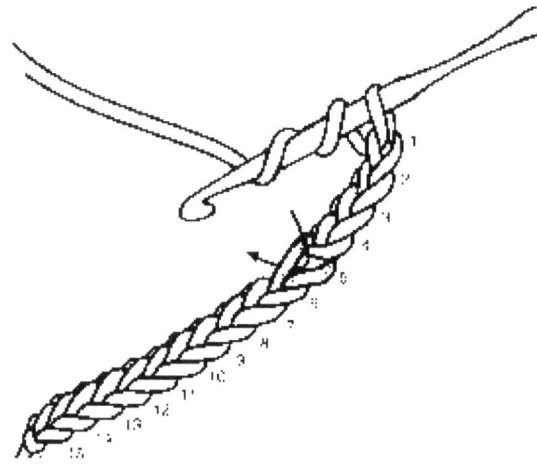

2. YO and draw it into the chain stitch and you will have four loops.

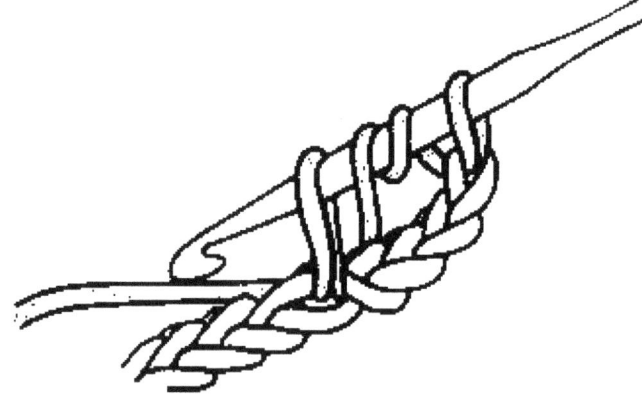

3. YO, draw through the first two loops and you will have three loops.

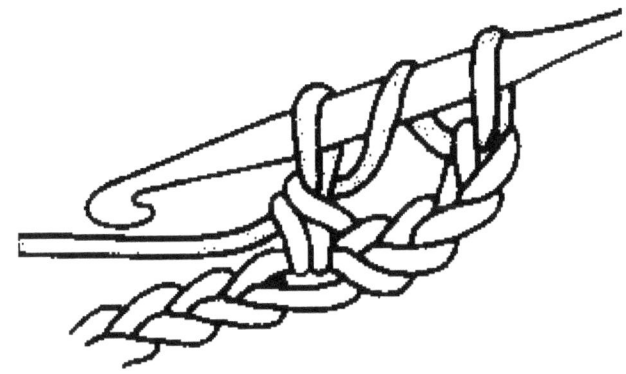

4. YO and into the first two loops on your hook and you will now have two loops.

5. YO and into the remaining two loops and you have a treble crochet.

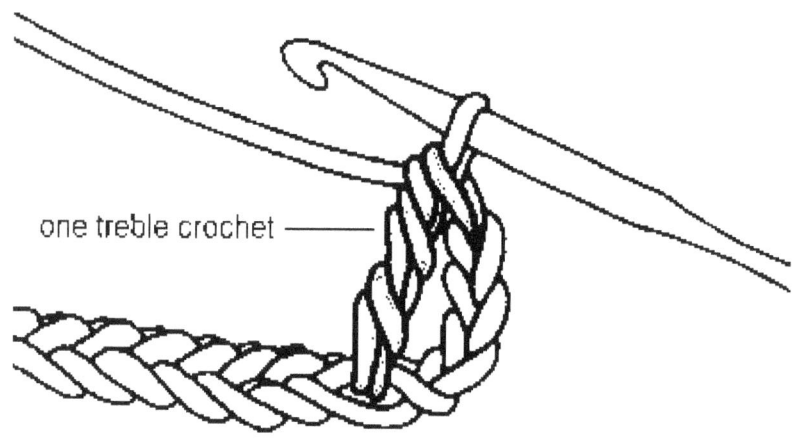

Easy Crochet Patterns for Beginners

1. Crochet Scarf

What you need

Yarn

Hook

Instructions

CH 62

Row 1: Do a half double crochet in the 3rd chain from the hook. Continue across with the HDCs to the end. CH 2 and turn.

Row 2: (Chain 2 also counts as a half double crochet) HDC across in every stitch. CH 2 and turn.

Row 3 – 7: Repeat row 2 and tie off

Note: Row 7 is where you can add another color if you want to give a small contrast

Seaming:

Make one twist in your scarf. Place both the flat and short ends together. Seam the 2 ends together with your long tail and tapestry needle. Weave in the ends and you are done.

2. Ribbed Boot Cuffs

What you need

Yarn

Yarn needle

5.50 mm/ I hook

Instructions

Gauge: 14 st x 17 r = 4" in back loop single crochet (blsc)

Ch 19

Row 1: Single crochet in the second chain from your hook and in each chain stitch across (18)

Row 2: Chain 1, turn and back loop single crochet in each stitch across (18)

Repeat row 2 until the piece measures 8" across (without being stretched) or until you achieve your desired length.

Ch 1 and insert the hook through the 1st stitch on both edges then slip stitch to join the edges of the boot cuff.

Repeat procedure all the way down the side. Cut the yarn and weave in the ends. Repeat to make the other boot cuff.

3. Leg Warmers

What you need

6 mm crochet hook

2-3 skeins

Darning needle

Scissors

Instructions

Ch 35

Join with a slip stitch to the 1st chain. Ensure that your chain is not twisted.

Row 1: Chain 3 and double crochet into each chain then join to the 3rd chain with a slip stitch.

Row 2-28: Chain 3 and double crochet into each stitch. Join to the third chain with a slip stitch.

Bind off and weave in the ends.

4. Crochet Washcloth

What you need

Any worsted weight yarn

Size k Hook

Scissors

Tapestry needle

Instructions

Ch 19

Row 1: Single crochet into the second chain from the hook and into each stitch across until the end, chain 1 and turn.

Row 2: Repeat until you obtain your desired width.

Cut the yarn and tie off. Use your tapestry needle to weave in the ends.

5. Crochet Coffee Sleeve

What you need

Chunky yarn

9mm N hook

Instructions

Row 1: Chain 20 and slip stitch to join

Rows 2-5: Chain 1 then half double crochet across the 20 stitches, and slip stitch to join

Row 6: Single crochet across and weave in the ends.

6. Blanket Scarf

What you need

11.5 mm hook

318-424 Yards of Bulky size 6 yarn

Instructions

Gauge: 6 stitches x 4 rows = 4×4 square

Length: 52 inches without the fringe

Row 1: Chain 28 then double crochet into the second chain until the last chain stitch, chain 2 then turn.

Row 2: Double crochet across, chain 2 and turn.

Repeat row 2 for 45 rows or until you achieve your desired length.

Finish off at the end of your last row and weave in ends.

7. Crochet Face Scrubbies

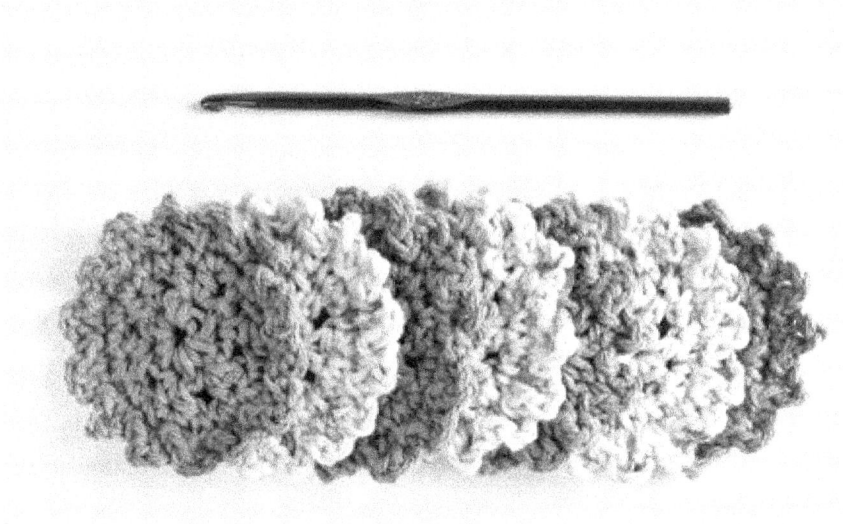

What you need

Yarn needle

5mm crochet hook

Worsted weight cotton yarn

Instructions

Chain 4 and join with a slip stitch to create a ring.

Row 1: Chain 2 then single crochet into the centre. (Chain 1 and single crochet into the centre) Repeat 4 times. Chain 2 then join to the 1st stitch with a slip stitch; you should now have a total of 12 stitches around the circle.

Row 2: Chain 2 (half double crochet 2 times into the gap from the previous round, chain 1) Repeat 5 times. Half double crochet into the gap formed from the previous round. Ch 1 then join into the 1st stitch with a slip stitch; you should now have 18 stitches around the circle.

Row 3: Chain 2 (single crochet, chain 1). Repeat 8 times. Single crochet 2 then join to the 1st stitch with a slip stitch; 27 stitches around the circle.

Row 4: Chain 1 (chain 3 and slip stitch into the next stitch, sc) Repeat 12 times. Chain 3 then slip stitch in the final stitch.

Secure the final stitch then weave in the ends with a yarn needle.

8. Washcloth Set Crochet Pattern

What you need

5.5 mm Hook

Worsted cotton yarn

Scissors

Tapestry needle

Instructions

Approximate dimensions 9.5" by 9.5"

Gauge: 2"= 5.5 single crochet

Ch 26

Row 1: Single crochet into the 2nd chain from your hook and into each stitch across.

Row 2: Chain 1 then turn and single crochet into each stitch across.

Row 3: Chain 1 then turn and single crochet into the first 2 stitches. *single crochet into the next stitch then double crochet into the following stitch; repeat from * across then single crochet into the last 3 stitches.

Row 4: Chain 1 then turn. Single crochet into the 1st stitch *single crochet into the next stitch then double crochet into the following stitch; repeat from * across then single crochet into the last 2 stitches.

Row 5-29: repeat rows 3 and 4.

Row 30-31: Chain 1 then turn. Single crochet into each stitch across

Cut the yarn ad tie off. Weave in all ends.

9. Men's Crochet Scarf

What you need

Light worsted weight wool yarn

6.5 mm hook

Instructions

16 stitches and 28 rows = 4inches in pattern

Approximate dimensions = 75" by 5"

Chain 301 (use stitch markers to mark every 25 stitches to keep track of the chain stitches since they are quite many).

Row 1: Slip stitch into the second chain from your hook and in each chain stitch across the row (300 slip stitches).

Row 2: Chain 1 then turn. Work on the entire row with slip stitches (300 slip stitches).

Row 3: Chain 1 then turn. Work on the entire row with slip stitches (300 slip stitches)

Row 4: Chain 1 then turn. Work on the entire row with single crochet (300 single crochet stitches)

Row 5: Chain 1 then turn. Work in slip stitches for the entire row in front loop only of the single crochet from the row below (300 slip stitches)

Row 6: Chain 1 then turn. Work in slip stitches for entire row (300 slip stitches)

Row 7: Chain 1 then turn. Work in slip stitches for entire row (300 slip stitches)

Row 8: Chain 1 then turn. Work in single crochet for entire row (300 single crochet stitches)

Repeat rows 5-8 until you achieve your desired scarf length. Ensure you end with 3 slip stitches rows

End off then weave in the ends.

10. Mug Rugs

What you need

Yarn needle

5 mm crochet hook

4.25 mm crochet hook

1 skein worsted weight cotton yarn

Scissors

Instructions

Main coaster

Row 1: Chain 8, single crochet in the second chain from your hook and in the following 6 chains (7 single crochet stitches).

Row 2: Chain 1 (doesn't count as a stitch through the entire project), single crochet in the 1st stitch and each stitch across (7 single crochet stitches).

Row 3-9: Repeat row 2 then knot off and cut the yarn.

Fringe ends

Cut 14 4" pieces of yarn. Take one piece of the yarn and fold in half to attach fringe. Insert into stitch using a crochet hook and pull up the cut piece. Bring the cut ends through the loop and pull until tight. Repeat across in every stitch on both ends then trim the ends to match.

11. Crochet Dishcloth

What you need

1 skein cotton yarn

I hook

Instructions

Chain 25

Row 1: Into the 3rd chain from your hook, half double crochet until the end of the foundation chain – you should now have 22 stitches across. Chain 2 and turn.

Row 2: Half double crochet 22 times, chain 2 then turn. Continue until you have 16 rows – don't fasten off.

Add a single crochet row all round the 4 sides of your cloth. Begin by putting one single crochet in the stitch you are working on now. Rotate the cloth in order to crochet down the left side.

Single crochet in each space down the side - It does not need to be exact, just ensure it is even as you go down otherwise your cloth will bunch.

12. Crochet Ear Warmer

What you need

5.00 mm hook

Tapestry needle

Scissors

Worsted weight yarn

Instructions

Chain 56

Row 1: Slip stitch into the first chain.

Row 2: Start working in rounds; chain 1 and half double crochet around then join to the first half double crochet.

Repeat row 2 until you have 8 rows – you can add more if desired.

Fasten off and leave a long tail.

To cinch the ear warmer, thread the tail into your yarn needle. Collect the seamed section of your headband and fold it into half ensuring that the fold is facing you.

Bring either of the sides to the top of your fold and secure it in place.

Run the needle through all the sections of the material you have gathered.

Wrap your yarn around the underside of your cinch then through the sections once more. Do this several times so that you secure the cinch, fasten the end and weave in the tail.

13. Color Block Bag

What you need

Darning needle

Scissors

Light worsted yarn- 3 colors

5.00 mm hook

4 metal D-rings

Instructions

Ch 54 with color A

Row 1: Single crochet into the 2nd chain from your hook and single crochet into every stitch across the row and chain 1.

Row 2-4: Single crochet in every stitch across the row then chain 1 and turn

Row 5-18: Single crochet, double crochet into the 1st stitch, skip a stitch, *single crochet, double crochet into the following stitch, skip a stitch * repeat* to the end - end with a single crochet in the last stitch. Chain 1 and turn.

Row 19-36: Change to color B. Single crochet then double crochet into the 1st stitch, skip a stitch, *single crochet then double crochet into the following stitch, skip a stitch *repeat* to the end, ending with a single crochet in the final stitch. Chain 1 and turn

Row 37-75: Change to color C. Single crochet then double crochet into the 1st stitch, skip a stitch, *single crochet then double crochet into the following stitch, skip a stitch *repeat* to the end, ending with a single crochet in the final stitch. Chain 1 and turn.

Row 76-92: Change to color B. Single crochet then double crochet into the 1st stitch, skip a stitch, *single crochet then double crochet into the following stitch, skip a stitch *repeat* to the end, ending with a single crochet in the final stitch. Chain 1 and turn

Row 93-106: Change to color A. Single crochet then double crochet into the 1st stitch, skip a stitch, *single crochet then double crochet into the following stitch, skip a stitch *repeat* to the end, ending with a single crochet in the final stitch. Chain 1 and turn

Row 107-110: Single crochet in each stitch across the row.

Cut the yarn and weave in the ends.

14. Fall Crochet Bunting

What you need

Size 4 yarn in two colors

6.0 mm hook

Scissors

Yarn needle

Instructions

Gauge: 4" across= 13 double crochet

Approximate dimensions: Each rectangle = 6.25" tall x 4.5 " wide

Row 1: 14 foundation double crochet using color A or Chain 16 then double crochet in the third chain from your hook and in every chain across (14).

Row 2: Chain 1 and turn. Single crochet in the same stitch and in every stitch across (14), Change to color B and finish off color A

Row 3: Chain 1 and turn. Single crochet in the same stitch and in every stitch across, Change to color A and finish color B (14).

Row 4: Chain 2 and turn. Double crochet in the same stitch and in every stitch across, Change to color B and finish color A (14)

Row 5: Chain 2 and turn. Double crochet in the same stitch and in every stitch across, Change to color A and finish color B (14).

Row 6: Chain 2 and turn. Double crochet in the same stitch and in every stitch across, Change to color B and finish color A (14).

Row 7: Chain 1 and turn. Single crochet in the same stitch and in every stitch across, Change to color A and finish color B (14). Complete the rest of the pattern with color A.

Row 8: Chain 1 and turn. Single crochet in the same stitch and in every stitch across (14).

Row 9: Chain 2 and turn. Double crochet in the same stitch and in every stitch across (14).

Rows 10-15: Repeat rows 8 and 9 (14).

Finish off and weave in all ends.

15. Crochet Pillow

What you need

Bulky weight yarn

6.5 mm crochet hook

Scissors

18" pillow insert

Yarn needle

Instructions

Row 1 (RS): Chain 48 – first 2 chains count as 1 double crochet, 1 double crochet in the third chain from your hook and in every chain across (47 dc)

Row 2: Chain 2 and turn, 1 front post double crochet into each stitch across – 47Front post double crochet.

Row 3: Chain 2 (counts as 1 double crochet) and turn, 1 double crochet in every stitch across – 47 double crochet.

Row 4-31: Repeat rows 2 to 3

Row 32: Repeat row 2

Fasten off the 1st piece after row 32. Don't fasten off the 2nd piece after row 32.

Finishing

With the wrong sides touching, hold the 2 pieces together. Proceeding from where you left off in the end of row 32 on the 2nd piece:

Chain 1, single crochet evenly around 3 sides going through both pieces, insert the pillow insert and proceed along the 4th side. Invisible join to the first single crochet and fasten off.

16. Baby blanket

What you need

Yarn

Tapestry needle

Stitch market

Size I crochet hook

Instructions

Gauge: 4 stitches = 1 inch

Chain 105 (these instructions are for a small size blanket

Row 1: Put a stitch marker in the 1st chain from the hook, single crochet in the third chain from hook (chain 1 then skip next stitch and single crochet in the following stitch). Repeat across the whole row then chain 1 and turn

Row 2: (Single crochet in the following stitch, chain 1, space, chain 1). Repeat this sequence in brackets across the remaining row. Work a single crochet stitch into the stitch where you had placed your marker at the end of the row. Remove the marker before you work on the stitch. Chain 1 and turn

Rows 3 and up: The remaining rows are all similar to row 2 apart from one minor difference at the end of the row: work the final single crochet stitch into the turning chain of the previous row. Keep repeating this row until you reach your desired length

Finishing

Cut the yarn leaving at least 6 inches of extra yarn. Use the yarn to thread the tapestry needle then weave the loose end of the yarn into the blanket.

Do the same with any other loose end hanging from the blanket (usually occurs when switching balls of yarn).

17. Tablet Cover

What you need

Light worsted yarn in 2 colors

5.00 mm crochet hook

Decorative button

Instructions

Row 1: Chain 27 with color 1, 3 sc in the second chain from your hook, make 1 sc in each of the following 24 chains, 6 single crochet in the final chain working on the opposite side of the cast on chain. Work 1 sc in each of the following 24 chains, 3 single crochet in the final chain, slip stitch to the 1st single crochet on the starting row. Turn (60 single crochet)

Row 2-4: Chain 1, make 1 single crochet in the base of chain 1 then 1 sc in each sc to finish, slip stitch to 1st single crochet then fasten off at the end of row 4.

Join in color 2

Row 1 (WS): Chain 2, make 1 double crochet at the base of chain 2, 1 double crochet in each stitch to end, slip stitch to the first double crochet on the starting row. Turn (60 double crochet)

Row 2(RS): Chain 1, make 1 single crochet in the base of chain 1 *front post double crochet around the following double crochet, make 1 single crochet in the following double crochet then repeat from * to *to end, slip stitch to the 1st single crochet on the starting row. Turn

Repeat pattern rows 1 and 2 two more times in color 2; there should now be 10 rows in all from the start. Fasten off

Repeat pattern rows 1 and 2 in colors as follows:

Color 3 three times, color 1 three times, color 2 three times – there should be 28 rows worked in all from the start

Join in color 3 and repeat pattern row 1

Button loop row: Chain 1, make 1 single crochet in the base of chain 1 *front post double crochet round the next double crochet, make 1 single crochet in the next double crochet, repeat from * to * until the last 14 double crochet. Make 1 single crochet in the next double crochet, chain 20, slip stitch to the final single crochet made then repeat from * to * to finish. Fasten off

Finishing

Thread the loose yarn around 2 small holes at each end, weave in the loose ends and trim, and attach the decorative button to the front cover to correspond with the button loop.

18. Chevron Crochet

What you need

Worsted weight yarn

Yarn needle

6.00 mm crochet hook

Scissors

Instructions

Begin by chaining a multiple of 17 then add 16 stitches to the length you chose (This pattern uses 33)

Row 1: Beginning in the 2nd chain from your hook single crochet 2 together, single crochet once in the following 5 stitches then make 3 single crochet (forms the hump) in the following stitch, *single crochet once in the following 7 stitches, skip the next 2 stitches. Single crochet once in the following 7 stitches, make 3 single crochet in the next stitch (hump) and repeat from * until you have 7 stitches remaining, single crochet once in the next 5 stitches and single crochet 2 together.

Row 2-your desired length: chain 1, repeat row 1

19. Newborn Crochet Bunny Hat (0-3 Months) – Without Ears

What you need

Tapestry needle

5.0 mm hook

2 small black buttons for the eyes

White worsted weight yarn

Any other color worsted weight yarn (I used pink)

Instructions

Magic ring: 11 double crochet in the magic ring then join to the first double crochet, chain 2.

Row 2: 2 double crochet in each around then join, chain 2 (22 dc).

Row 3: 2 double crochet in first stitch, double crochet in the next, rpt around then join, chain 2 (33 double crochet).

Row 4: 2 double crochet in 1st, double crochet in the next 2, rpt around then join, chain 2 (44 double crochet).

Row 5-10: double crochet in each round then join, chain 2 (44 double crochet).

Row 11: Single crochet in each around then join. Fasten off and weave in the ends (44 single crochet)

Mouth and nose: Use a tapestry needle and yarn to stitch on the nose and mouth. Just weave the yarn into an upside down triangle shape and a single line with 2 curves at the bottom. Do not over think this, it's quite simple.

20. Bunny Ears/ Cat Ears/ Pig Ears (Make 2)

What you need

2 colors worsted weight yarn

5.0 mm hook

Tapestry needle

Instructions

Chain 5, in the second chain from the hook make single chain in each across, chain 1 and turn (4 single crochet)

Row 2: 2 sc in 1st stitch, single crochet in the next 2 sc, 2 sc in the final stitch, chain 1 and turn (6 sc).

Row 3: Sc in each stitch across, chain 1 and turn (6 sc).

Row 4: 2 sc in the 1st stitch, single crochet in the following 4 stitches, 2 sc in the final stitch, chain 1 and turn (8 sc).

Rows 5-10: Sc in each stitch across, chain 1 and turn (8 sc) – you can continue to make rows of single crochet to make your ears longer (remember that the longer you make the ear, the floppier it will be).

Row 11: Single crochet decrease, single crochet in the following 4 stitches, single crochet decrease in the final stitch, chain 1 and turn.

Row 12: Sc in each stitch across, chain 1 and turn (6 single crochet)

Row 13: Single crochet decrease, single crochet in the following 2 stitches, single crochet decrease in the final stitch, chain 1 and turn.

Row 14: Sc in each stitch across, chain 1 and turn (4 single crochet)

Row 15: Make 2 sc decreases, chain 1 and turn

Row 16: Single crochet decrease, chain 1 and keep making single crochet around the edge of the whole ear. Slip stitch to first single crochet to join. Leave a long tail to sew the ears together

Inside ear (make 2)

Follow the pattern above with a pink color (or your accent color). Make your single crochet decrease when you get to row 16 then switch the color to white and continue to make sc around the whole ear

With the long tail and your tapestry needle, sew the ears together and weave in and out under the edges with the sc. If desired, you can use pipe cleaner to help the ears stand up.

21. Chunky Crochet Blanket

What you need

Bulky weight yarn

15 mm crochet hook

Scissors

Yarn needle

Instructions

Row 1: 85 foundation single crochet, turn.

Row 2: Chain 3, 4 double crochet in same stitch. *skip 1 single crochet, double crochet in the following single crochet, rpt from * 6 times. Skip 1 single crochet, 5 double crochet in the following 2 single crochets. *skip 1 single crochet, double crochet in the following single crochet, rpt from * 6 times. Skip 1 single crochet, 5 double crochet in the following 2 single crochet. *skip 1 single crochet, double crochet in the following single crochet, repeat from * 6 times. Skip 1 single crochet, 5 double crochet in the following 2 single crochet. Skip 1 single crochet, double crochet in the following single crochet, rpt from *6 times, skip 1 single crochet, 5 double crochet in the following single crochet. Turn.

Row 3: Chain 1, single crochet in each stitch across working in the front loops only (85). Turn.

Repeat rows 2-3 until you achieve your desired length. Finish off and weave in the ends.

22. Vintage Coaster Pattern

What you need

4 mm hook

Cotton yarn

Instructions

pattern is written in UK terms

*3 chain counts as 1 treble

Row 1: magic ring, 3 chain (counted as 1 treble) 19 treble into the ring, join with slip stitch to the top of the starting chain 3 (20 treble).

Row 2: 3 chain, 1 treble in the following stitch, 2 chain, * 1 treble into each of the following 2 stitches, 2 chain and rpt from *around, join with slip stitch to the top, chain 3 (20 treble).

Row 3: Slip stitch into the next chain 2 sp, 3 chain, (1 treble, 2 chain, 2 treble) in the same sp, *(2 treble, 2 chain, 2 treble) into the following chain 2 sp, rpt from *around, join with slip stitch to the top of the starting chain 3 (40 treble).

Round 4: Slip stitch across into the following chain 2 sp, 3 chain, treble in the same sp then skip the next 2 treble, 1 double crochet in the sp before the next 2 treble, *7 treble in the following chain 2 then skip 2 treble, 1 double crochet in the space and rpt from *around, join with slip stitch to the top of the starting chain 3 – you should now have 10 petals made from 7 treble clusters each of which are separated with 1 dc.

23. Chain Stitch Crochet Necklace

What you need

Yarn

Hook

Yarn needle

Instructions

Chain and keep chaining until the piece can make a loop of the size you prefer for your necklace. Once you think the chain is the correct length for one loop hold the end on your hook and the starting end together to see what it looks like – you can even try it on to see whether the length satisfies you.

Attach a marker if you have one.

Keep making your chain until it is long enough to make 3 loops then check whether you like it. If not, just keep going. Each time you make a chain enough for another loop look at it to ensure you like the number of loops you make. Clip yarn and pull the end through.

Wrap and tie: Lay the necklace down then tie the beginning and end together. To even out the loops, place your hands inside the necklace and stretch (optional). Wrap each end of your yarn in opposite directions around your necklace then tie it tight to hold all loops together.

Band: Cut some yarn (approx. 4 feet long) and put the yarn into a tapestry needle on one end. Sew through the bundle you had tied the loops together to leave about a 2" tail. Leave at least half an inch from your knot then begin wrapping around the loops, working over the knot and end at least ½" away from the knot in the other side. Do not cut the yarn and do not be alarmed if some loops are showing through. Wrap yarn around the back in the other direction to make a second layer. If you want, you can make a 3rd layer. Sew the end of the yarn back and forth through the wrapped section. Clip all ends of yarn.

24. Crochet Cuffed Baby Booties (6-12 Months)

What you need

Medium worsted weight yarn in two colors

4.00 mm hook

Yarn needle

Buttons

Instructions

Begin with color 1

Ch 10, single crochet in the second chain from the hook, single crochet in the next 7 and make 5 single crochet in the final chain.

Turn to work on the opposite side and single crochet 8, join, chain 2.

Row 2: Hdc, 2 hdc, hdc in the following 6, 2 hdc in the following 2, half double crochet in the next 2, 2 half double crochet in the next 2, half double crochet in the following 6, 2 half double crochet, half double crochet in the last, join and chain 1.

Row 3: Single crochet 10, 2 single crochet in the next, 2 half double crochet in the following 5, 2 single crochet in the next 2, single crochet in the next 10, join and chain 1.

Row 4: Only in the back loops, single crochet around, join and chain 1 (39 single crochet).

Row 5: Only in the back loops, single crochet around, join and chain 1 (40 single crochet).

Now using color 2

Row 6: Single crochet around ensuring you make the stitches deep (40 single crochet).

Row 7: Now working on both loops, single crochet around, join and chain 1 (40 single crochet).

Row 8: Single crochet 12, (single crochet decrease, single crochet in the following 2) 4 times then single crochet 12, join and chain 1.

Row 10: Single crochet 10, make 6 single crochet decreases, single crochet 11, join and chain 1.

Round 11: Single crochet 10, make 3 single crochet decreases, single crochet 11, join and chain 1.

Row 12: Single crochet 10, make 2 single crochet decreases, single crochet 10, join and chain 1.

Row 13-16: Single crochet around, join and chain 1, (22 single crochet) (change color at the end of round 16).

Go back to using color 1

Row 17: Single crochet around in the new color, join and chain 1 (22 single crochet).

Row 18: Half double crochet around (total 22 half double crochet).

Row 19: Single crochet around (total 22 single crochet).

Row 20: Half double crochet around (total 22 half double crochet)

Row 21: Single crochet around (total 22 single crochet)

Row 22: Half double crochet around (total 22 half double crochet)

Fasten off and weave in the loose ends.

Fold over the cuff (row 17 to 22)

Optional: you can create a thicker rim by making a slip stitch around the bottom

Tiny 5 petal flower pattern

Make a magic ring, single crochet 10 in the ring, join and chain 1

In the next stitch (half double crochet, double crochet, half double crochet) all in one stitch, chain 1 and slip stitch to the next stitch, chain 1 – repeat around

Finish off and leave a tail to sew on.

25. Cotton Crochet Throw Blanket

What you need

Yarn- 2 colors, black and white

J Hook

Yarn needle

Instructions

Black stripe

Chain 115 with black yarn and the J hook.

Row 1: Use the H hook, to dc into the fourth chain from your hook. Dc into every stitch to the end (112 stitches), turn.

Row 2: Chain 3, double crochet into every stitch (112 stitches).

Rows 3-6: Rpt row 2 – if using small balls of yarn, this should almost use it all up and leave a generous tail to weave in. Trim the yarn if using a large ball and leave about 6 inches to weave in later

White stripe

Double crochet 6 white crochet rows as above.

Rpt, alternating between the both colors until you achieve your desired length.

Weave in the ends as you go.

Common Mistakes in Crochet and How to Avoid Them

Let us now look at some common mistakes in crochet and ways of dealing with them:

Your project getting wider and wider

Every crocheter makes this common mistake at least once. Being new to crocheting, you may think that it's all about repeating the same stitch back and forth then as you begin working on a rectangle blanket, you realize an hour later that it has now turned to a hexagon.

This issue normally occurs when you crochet without counting stitches and you end up with more stitches than required. You could be unintentionally working a stitch in the turning chain or doubling up into one stitch.

The only way to avoid this mistake is by counting your stitches. You could count each row as you complete one or stay keen on the shape of your work. There is no need for you to waste your time working quickly and then realize you added an extra stitch.

Only crocheting in the front loop

It is easy to make this mistake when you are new to crochet. It is very important to learn where you are supposed to place the hook in every stitch; in fact, it is the basis of the craft.

Spending some time analyzing each row, as you work is an effective way of fixing this mistake. It might be tiresome but is much better than having to crochet wrongly.

Using the wrong hook size

Using the wrong hook size can dramatically alter the outcome of the project. Each crochet pattern is usually written with a specific size of hook in mind and changing it can make your stitches either too loose or too tight. Ensure that you read your pattern well in order to be sure you are using the correct hook size. Also, make your gauge swatch as well. Sometimes, you might not know that you are using the wrong hook and once you see the gauge swatch is off then you save yourself from wasting time ruining the whole project.

Not knowing where to put the first stitch/not counting the starting chain correctly

As earlier mentioned, the starting chain is the backbone of each crochet project – it's probably also the least enjoyable part of a project. When crocheting, learning to make a chain is among the first things you will learn and it can be quite confusing.

When doing a foundation chain, a common mistake is not putting your first stitch in the right chain. This results in either not enough or too many stitches and if you are not counting these stitches, then your project is doomed. The best way to fix or avoid this problem is to familiarize yourself with how to count the chains and how to chain.

US/UK term confusion

When looking for new patterns to try out, you should check whether the crocheting instructions are from the UK or the US since the terminology differs slightly. For example, "double crochet" means something different to those in the US than it does to the crocheters in the UK. The table below shows the UK equivalent to US stitching terms.

US/Canada Stitch Names	UK/Australia/Europe Stitch Names
Slip Stitch (sl st)	Slip Stitch (sl st) (or simply stitch)
Single Crochet (sc)	Double Crochet (dc)
Double Crochet	Treble/Triple Crochet
Triple Crochet	Double-treble

The following chapter will focus on some tips to make your crocheting experience better.

Crochet Tips for Beginners

Let us look at some tips that will make crocheting easier for you especially as a beginner:

Pick up your hook everyday

The hardest part about learning how to crochet is training your hand to hold your hook (and the yarn) with the correct tension. At first, it feels a little awkward and unnatural but if you make it a habit of picking up your hook everyday when you are first learning the craft; it will become easy in no time. Do not give up and keep in mind that practice makes perfect!

Begin with small projects

Learning how to crochet takes time and most of the times, beginners feel discouraged when they are not able to complete a project – I mean, who wouldn't? The best thing to do is to start with small attainable projects. There is no better feeling than completing your very own first project. Start with small items such as squares, mandalas and coasters before moving onto larger projects such as blankets and cushions

Chain, chain, chain

When learning to crochet, making several chains is the best way to improve your tension since they are the foundation of all stitches. You will be ready for stitches that are more complicated once all your chains look nice and even

Make stitch swatches

You can work on small swatches to help you to familiarize yourself with the different stitches. You can even sew these swatches together to create face cloths or small blankets.

Avoid Changing Hooks in the Middle of a Project

Your stitches should be consistent throughout the whole project. When you switch hooks mid-project, you risk creating an inconsistency. Even changing same size hooks from one manufacture to another can be problematic. This is because the size of the hook is not always the same between manufacturers and small change in how the hooks are shaped can change the way you create your stitches or hold the hook hence the need of practice swatches.

Conclusion

We have come to the end of the book. Thank you for reading and congratulations for reading until the end!

If you found the book valuable, can you recommend it to others? One way to do that is to post an honest review.

Thank you and good luck!